READING THE SIGNS OF THE TIMES

A Prophetic Response to Jamaica @ 60

STEPHEN C.A. JENNINGS

CHRIST Publishing

Kingston, Jamaica

CHRIST Publishing

Copyright © 2022 by CHRIST Publishing

All rights reserved, including the right to reproduce this book or portions thereof in any form whatsoever.

In memory of my parents Clyde, and Molly Jennings

Contents

Acknowledgements	i
Introduction	v
Describing	1
Discerning	9
Doing	13
Summary	26

Acknowledgements

I praise and thank Almighty God, Father, Son, and Spirit, who inspired this work, and who gave us the opportunity to share God's word with the world.

I thank my wife, Dione, for her love, support and ideas that helped make this book stronger. Special thanks to our children, Daniel, Arielle, and Gabrielle. Their regular encouragement to their Dad to "write your books so our generation might get yours," motivated me to get this work out. I hope this is the first of many for them and their peers.

Gratitude to my siblings, Mark, Grace, and Lois, and their families, for helpful reflections on present day Jamaica, and how it changed since our days as children. I thank my wife's siblings and their families for ongoing support in this project. My father- and mother-in-law, Basil and Cherry White, deserve special mention for their continual exhortations and prayers for success of this work.

I thank the Jamaica Baptist Union (JBU) for the opportunity to present the 2022 David Jelleyman Lectures, on which this book is based. That lecture series is named for a British Baptist Missionary who, for 46 years, along with his wife, Christine, gave sterling service to the JBU in particular, and the Jamaican church in general. The lecture series reflects on contemporary issues from a biblical-theological perspective. I wrote this work with that approach and hope that I accurately represented the intentions of the JBU, as well as the scholarly spirit of Rev. and Mrs. Jelleyman.

I thank the Mona and Mammee River Baptist Churches, which I pastor, for their prayerful support. Thanks too, to members of the JBU and others who gave important feedback to the initial presentation. I hope this book gives them much to think about and give us further impetus in our God-given ministry and mission.

I thank the Rev. Eron Henry, JBU minister and Communications and Media Manager for the Lott Carey Society, for his editorial and publishing expertise. His patient and persistent guidance helped move this work forward to become what it is. I also thank Rev. Brenard McDonald, JBU minister, pastor of the Grace Baptist Church, May Pen, and graphic artist extraordinaire, for his cover design. He took my embryonic ideas and made them into the excellent book cover we have. Thanks too, to Mrs. Jolyn Gayle, who transcribed and proofread the early texts of the first drafts of this work.

Finally, I thank all who read and listen to this book, particularly those who love Jamaica and who identify with its promise and potential. I pray you will find it helpful, and that it will assist us as God's people to understand the times and situations in which we live and stimulate us to act.

I dedicate this book to the memory of my parents, Clyde and Molly Jennings. Both were outstanding ministers of the gospel, Dad as a pastor, Mom as a nurse.

Dad was not just an outstanding pastor, but an outstanding parent. He taught my siblings and I to read, and the first book we learned to read from was the Bible. As one descended from fisherfolk, he taught me how to read the weather. To discern the signs of the time in weather patterns. He taught me to play dominoes and to learn how to read the

game. Often, when I had the domino pieces in my hand for a while, he would say, "Don't just read the game, son. Do something!" From him, I owe the perspective that *analysis* ought to be matched by *action*. I thank him for being the first to teach me how to read the Bible with one hand, and read the news – newspapers, radio, television, and the conversations of ordinary people – with the other hand.

Dad died last year, 2021, a few days after celebrating his 60th anniversary as an ordained minister of the Jamaica Baptist Church, while Mom passed a few years ago. This year, 2022, they would have celebrated their 60th wedding anniversary, a few days before Jamaica celebrate its 60th anniversary of independence. I hope they would be proud of this work, and of their firstborn son.

July 2022

Introduction

Jamaica @ 60
Jamaica turns 60 this year, 2022. In August 1962, the country became an independent nation. It ceased being a colony of Britain and became sovereign over its own affairs. Much has changed since the Jamaican people set out on the formal path of national self-determination. It is therefore, useful to reflect on and respond to what Jamaica has become in the season of its diamond anniversary. I ask that we "read the signs of the times" in relation to Jamaica and Jamaicans.

Explaining, Exegeting and Expositing "Reading the Signs of the Times"
The title of this book is *Reading the Signs of the Times*. The phrase "reading the signs of the times" comes from passages of scripture from Jesus, God's Messiah from Nazareth, that are recorded in three of the four Gospels. Particularly, it comes from Matthew 16:1-4:

> 16 The Pharisees and Sadducees came to Jesus and tested him by asking him to show them a sign from heaven.
>
> [2] He replied, 'When evening comes, you say, "It will be fair weather, for the sky is red,"
>
> [3] and in the morning, "Today it will be stormy, for the sky is red and overcast." You know how to interpret

the appearance of the sky, but you cannot interpret the signs of the times.[a]

⁴ A wicked and adulterous generation looks for a sign, but none will be given it except the sign of Jonah.' Jesus then left them and went away. (NIV)

The Good News Translation makes it even more clear what was going on:

16 Some Pharisees and Sadducees who came to Jesus wanted to trap him, so they asked him to perform a miracle for them, to show that God approved of him.

²But Jesus answered, "When the sun is setting, you say, 'We are going to have fine weather, because the sky is red.'

³ And early in the morning you say, 'It is going to rain, because the sky is red and dark.' You can predict the weather by looking at the sky, but you cannot interpret the signs concerning these times

⁴ How evil and godless are the people of this day! You ask me for a miracle? No! The only miracle you will be given is the miracle of Jonah."

So he left them and went away.

Jesus was telling the Pharisees and Sadducees, "You are asking for a sign, yet you can tell what's going on around you. You can read and even predict the weather, but you cannot read the signs of the times. The only signs you will get is the

sign of Jonah, my resurrection from the dead after three days." And he leaves them.

Luke 12:54-57 says Jesus spoke not only to the Pharisees and Sadducees, which is what Matthew and Mark highlight, but He also spoke to the people in general:

> ^{54} Jesus said also to the people, "When you see a cloud coming up in the west, at once you say that it is going to rain—and it does.
>
> ^{55} And when you feel the south wind blowing, you say that it is going to get hot—and it does.
>
> ^{56} Hypocrites! You can look at the earth and the sky and predict the weather; why, then, don't you know the meaning of this present time?
>
> ^{57} "Why do you not judge for yourselves the right thing to do? (GNT)

Jesus was saying: "You who are looking for signs and wonders and all kinds of miracles; there's a place for that, but you are focusing so much on the spectacular you're missing the ordinary everyday things around you. You can tell what will happen with the weather when there is a change; when it will be hot or hotter than before; when it will rain more than before. You can tell if it will be hot because you don't feel the wind and you can tell if it will rain because the wind is coming from another direction. **And yet you can't tell what is happening now. And you can't even do what is right.** Why don't you do what is right? Why don't you figure out things to

put your life in order so when things happen you are not caught off guard?"

That is what Jesus meant by reading the signs of the times.

While Jesus spoke with His people about what was happening in their time, I believe the Scriptures advise hearers/readers of every era to "read the signs" of their times. We need to "read the signs" of our time, to understand what is happening now and do what is right in relation to what's going on. We read these signs through the prism of the Scriptures, with Jesus as our Teacher and the Holy Spirit as our Enabler. I pay particular attention to "reading the signs of these times" in relation to Jamaica, to understand what is happening now and do what is right in relation to what's going on, with the help of the Holy Spirit of Jesus.

Having seen the meaning of Jesus' phrase of "reading the signs of the times," let us look at Jamaica as we read the signs of the times, much as we would "read" the weather and/or read a game of dominoes. To do so we need to do three things. First, to describe the times, i.e., to figure out what is happening; second, to discern the times, i.e., to figure out why what is happening is happening; and thirdly to do something about the times, i.e., to act on what we know about the times, more precisely, to act in light of the times.

Describing

Concrete Development and Cultural Confidence

Jamaica is a place of concrete development and cultural confidence. Across Jamaica there is evidence of building and construction. From apartments and housing solutions to highways and roads, to businesses and information, and computer technologies such as tablets, cell phones and the Internet. There is evidence of change and growth. We compare this to 60 years ago when Jamaica was newly independent. Many changes have taken place. Jamaicans have greater access to one another and to the world at large.

Accompanying that is a greater cultural confidence. Jamaicans are less ashamed of who they are and how they look. More Jamaicans speak the Jamaican language, so-called Patois, more easily, unrestrained in public, than they did in the late 60s to the early 70s. More people wear Afrocentric hairstyles such as braids, twists, and locs than they did prior to the 70s. Music and arts have become the face of Jamaica to the world. Where there was always folk music, such as Mento, since the Reggae revolution of the 70s, Jamaica is known and recognized for its contribution to World music via Ska, Rock Steady, Reggae and Dancehall. These gave birth to other Black music, such as Hip Hop, Rap, Reggaeton and Afrobeats.

Jamaica's contribution to sports, particularly in track and field, has established us as a world powerhouse and has made our sense of global significance more substantial. We could argue truthfully that Jamaica and Jamaicans have come a long

way culturally, particularly when one compares our present to our early years.

Crime and Corruption

That said, Jamaica is in a contradictory space. While there is much to celebrate, there is also much to remonstrate. Jamaica is marked by crime and corruption. While some crime level perhaps is inevitable because of human beings and their sinful tendencies, crime in Jamaica, especially homicides and white-collar crime, are on the increase. This is not merely anecdotal but can be seen from the latest crime statistics. (See Charts 1 & 2)

Corruption seems to be endemic in the system, whether governmental apparatuses, or private sector entities. Even religious bodies such as the church. Corruption has become such a part of Jamaican life that it is seen by many as normal to steal, curry favour, bribe or to take a cut. Whenever some people in the country quarrel or argue about corruption, their only complaint is who is more corrupt than the other. Not whether corruption is a problem. Indeed, one person's corruption is another person's favour.

Capital-Driven Society

But what drives this crime and corruption? There are many reasons, but one is that Jamaica, like other places in the world, has become a Capital-Driven Society. The major engine of growth is money and the making of more money. Not only at the expense of other people's labour, but of the land, waterways, seas, and the atmosphere. Because of this, people are driven to get more money for themselves and their family.

Community and Character Fragmentation
Consequently, there are other things taking place. This has led to what I call Community and Character Fragmentation. Communities are breaking down physically and socially because of the injection, or the desire for the injection of capital. Villages that were at the heart of Jamaica are being penetrated, for instance, by mining to produce income for investors. Those who once occupied these hitherto gathered communities, are scattered across the country and across the world with little or no social cohesion. Thus, people who were once close together physically and psychologically are now farther apart.

This caused greater pressure on the minds and spirits of persons who feel more acutely their individuality. Such persons feel anxious, worried, and depressed because they lack certainty about the future. They are misplaced and are without certain forms of support. Many struggle with mental challenges and some become mentally ill, sometimes without knowing it.

Climate Crisis
Capital-driven societies have contributed to the global climate crisis in general and Jamaica in particular. With the removal of the trees and the topsoil for agricultural purposes, building, and mining, and with the blockage of drains, run-offs, and waterways in the name of construction, natural occurrences such as rainfall become hazards, resulting in flooding, loss of life and property. Such practices contribute to droughts,

disturbing the water cycle and affecting agriculture, food security and general well-being. Water is life. There is the overharvesting of the seas as more people seek to eat healthily, but at the expense of sea creatures and of the sea itself.

It is not only the sea that is affected or on the line, but the air also. In the name of production, pollution of the atmosphere occurs, whether through factories or the exhaust of motor vehicles or other machines. In short, the entire country – and planet – is affected adversely by the activities of capital-driven societies.

COVID-19

The activities of capital-driven societies is seen in the advent of COVD-19 and its handling by governments across the world. The origins of COVID are debated. The debate centres around those who assert it was made in a lab. However, early on, it was stated it started through transmission of viruses from animals to humans in wet markets in China. Those animals were for the diets of elite Chinese and were seen as status food. If so, it was the tastes of these wealthy Chinese that inadvertently led to animals passing the virus to human. Simply put, COVID-19 could have been a rich person-initiated disease.

But it is in its handling globally that revealed how wealth often determines health. The richer countries of the world often bought and hoarded vaccines for themselves, while poorer countries could not afford or did not have access to them. Even within richer countries, many poorer persons were initially unable to access basic healthcare including masks, oxygen, and vaccines. Such strategies backfired because these

countries discovered the hard way that persons are always interacting with other persons and that *viruses have no nationality*. Keeping one's country safe from other countries and peoples of other countries is a global impossibility.

In Jamaica, our problem was not accessibility of vaccines but what COVID-19 revealed about our country. COVID revealed how fragmented Jamaica is, the clear and many differences between persons living in the same country. Gaps and differences in income. Economic differences showing some accessed income whether or not they came out for their jobs, while others had to hustle and even break the COVID-19 restrictions to survive.

Differences were seen in opportunities as some people had access to technology – tablets, computers, Wi-Fi – while others did not have access to these things. This opened gaps educationally and revealed the real differences between people in terms of education and opportunities for learning. Some were able to be online and go to school continually, while others could not go to school. Some remained in school, while others dropped out of school. Some used the technologies; others lacked the knowhow.

This also revealed real differences in people's social standing. It was clear that some people had access to resources while others were unable to access basic resources.

However, COVID-19 revealed a more fundamental difference, namely in the understandings between people. Not so much about persons' intelligence or knowledge, but outlook and worldview. To cite a basic example: In Jamaica as well as elsewhere, we see differences people had with science and religion, and their relationship to each other. For some

persons, religion and science are partners, and religion ought to support the science. For others, religion and science are adversaries, so science is against religion and religion is therefore against the science. The differences among the Jamaican and global population as to who to trust reveals fundamental differences among individuals. "Whose report will we believe?" people ask, even as the debate about "to be vaccinated or not to be vaccinated" rages.

Worse, the differences people naturally have in our society became divisions. There are few attempts to have civil discussions to see each other's point of view, to meet each other part way, to try to meet in the middle. Instead of decent debate, we have acrimonious discussions, hostile condemnation, and dismissive argumentation. Elements of the church community sadly led the charge on one side or the other. This is another sign of how fragmented current Jamaican community is.

Church Ineffectiveness: Cult-like Behaviours and Changing Demographics

The biggest challenge in Jamaica is the relative ineffectiveness of the church. It is not that the church does nothing. It is not dealing with some of the fundamental issues in Jamaican society. For instance, the church is not a part of the concrete development of the society. It is not building roads nor apartments other than church buildings. It is a beneficiary of Information and Computer Technologies rather than the originator of these products, and has used these products, especially in these COVID-19 times, to good effects. But it is not dealing with the shadowy usage of these things, nor is the

church engaging with community and character fragmentation, climate crisis or crime and corruption.

The church's involvement in society assists in meeting the material wellbeing of the Jamaican people. However, its engagement is often stuck in the mode of charity, giving specific goods and services to the poor and needy. It sometimes initiates a few development projects such as skills training, rather than fundamental liberating operations that enable the poor and needy to free themselves from the shackles of poverty. Worse, the church is not involved in the radical transformation of society that creates a more just and life-giving place where people live, work, and raise their families. The church is not making the impact to transform the family, nation, and people of Jamaica.

This is exacerbated by and is exacerbating a cult-like behaviour by some Jamaicans who make themselves inerrant, invincible, and indispensable, whose authority and knowledge of the will of God is near omniscient. Other Jamaicans believe such cultic-church leaders should never be questioned but obeyed. In a recent incident, one cultic-church leader, an Apostle, told one church member to "sacrifice" another to avert divine wrath, which the member promptly did. The police arrested both pastor and member for murder. Alas, the Apostle died before he could be tried in court. Though this is an extreme case, other church leaders behave in cultic ways. In the name of the Lord, they "decree" what is to be done by their members. Some members blithely follow the path they are led on in their quest for personal peace and prosperity.

Another basic problem contributes to societal ineffectiveness of the church in Jamaica: the changing

demographics of the church. The percentage of those who identify with Christianity fell from 69 percent to 65 percent. Those identifying with another, or no religions, increased to 35 percent from 31 percent. Fewer men and fewer young people under the age of 35 identify with the Christian religion in 2021 as compared to 2011 and 2001. Interestingly, 83 percent of the population considered themselves either deeply and/or somewhat religious, though the number who are not much and/or were not religious (17 percent), increased in 2021, compared to previous census years. Christianity in its organised, official manner in Jamaica is less influential than it used to be. Many people are spiritual and believe in God, but do not believe in formal religions and churches. If the trends continue, Christianity will become more ineffective in Jamaican society. It is fragmented and lacks penetration. It risks becoming irrelevant because of a failure to engage youth, men, and more women in pertinent spiritual ways.

What can be done by the church to deal with these fundamental problems? To answer, we must do more digging. More precisely, we need to discern the reasons for these issues, specifically the capital-driven society and its malfeasant symptoms.

We now turn to the second section, "Discerning the Reasons for the Signs of the Times."

Discerning

International Colonial Legacies
Societies such as Jamaica are as they are because of the legacies of international colonialism. Jamaica was occupied for more than fifteen hundred years by First Nation peoples, such as the Tainos, also known as Arawak. When Europeans, led by the Spanish, came in 1494, they introduced colonialism. These territories were a source of extraction, exploitation, and extortion. The aim was to get as much as possible to increase riches in the conquering colonizing countries.

Jamaica was a means of making wealth, whether providing gold, as was first thought by the Spaniards, or tobacco, sugar, coffee, and bananas. Even after slavery was abolished in 1838, colonisation continued until 1962. After independence there were and are treaties to ensure preferential treatment to the former colonizing countries to ensure they have the advantage in international trade. We have legacies of that colonial arrangement, what we do or have to do, including trade and monetary arrangements.

Interconnected Imperialism
These legacies morphed into interconnected imperialism. The technologies that connect us to one another also connect us to the world around us. While this would be good, the deeper motive for it is not as good, which is to connect and to give access to the drivers of capital, whose aim is to make money at the expense of the majority of the planet's inhabitants and the planet itself. Not only are there former colonial actors and

agents seeking to enrich themselves, but there are also newer players, some local, seeking to do the same.

Inequality and Inequity

This resulted in great inequity and an increasing inequality within the country and across the world. The true statistics are hard to find, but the country's minimum wage is $7,500 per week or $30,000 a month. What many business owners and managers get in comparison shows a wide gap. In the late to mid-90s, a survey discovered that Jamaica had one of the biggest income gaps in the Caribbean. The bottom part of the social pyramid earned 200 percent less than the top part. One imagines where it is now, 30 years later. Inequality refers to the fact that people do not have the same income levels, nor purchasing power in numerical terms. Inequity refers to the unfair, preventable practices that affect persons' life chances, expectations and relationships, the hidden factors behind the inequality that is seen numerically.

Injustice and Iniquity

In Jamaica, like elsewhere, there is much injustice and inequality. Injustice because people are treated unfairly. They do not have the same opportunities as others even though they have the same needs, perhaps more. Iniquity is people reacting to this injustice meted out on them, perhaps by turning to crime or corruption, or by becoming depressed and distressed, acting out in antisocial and immoral ways.

Indifference and Idolatry

What is the reaction to this? For the average person, even the average Christian, unless people are personally affected, there is indifference to the plight of others. Charity is given to others, even prayers, but there is no passion to help change the situations that make the lives of individuals and groups persistently poor. When people pray, praise, and testify, at the heart of many forms of worship is to acquire this world's goods and services. When they do, or to make it happen, they make demands of God or claims in God's name. When carefully examined, such behaviours are forms of idolatry. We make gods of ourselves and our demands, and our chief goal is the worship of material things. We entreat the Living God as an object to supply our needs rather than a person to respond to in discipleship and obedience. Our service, prayer, and worship are about us rather than God, the supreme idolatry.

Identity Crisis

I believe the church in Jamaica, perhaps Jamaica itself, given its spiritual and theological history, is facing an identity crisis. The church has forgotten who it is and whose it is. That we were meant to be called people of God, chosen as signs and agents of the Kingdom of God among earth's people. That we are meant to be followers of Jesus Christ who in word, attitude, and deed show the glory of God by making differences that can be measured in practical, tangible ways in the lives of real people facing real situations. Instead, we are caught up in a mode of survival, trying to maintain church through religiosity, rather than being effective in the lives of the many who need

it. The country, overall, is losing its way because it is moving away from the spiritual roots that gave it greatness.

Imminent Judgement

For these and other reasons, the world, the country, and the church face imminent judgement. The Lord God is examining the planet and its component parts, including this country, under scrutiny. Through the various symptoms and situations – crime and violence, crime and corruption, community fragmentation, and COVID-19 – the Lord is examining the practices and the principles that characterise human societies to determine if they are treating citizens and strangers well and fairly or are doing the opposite.

Jesus said in Matthew 25 the Lord will judge people how they treated the naked stranger, and the hungry. This is not confined to the Last Judgement, but to whenever judgement is. Jamaica is facing judgement that is both local and global, presented in Revelation 3:10 as the "time of trouble which is coming upon the world to test all the people on earth."

As 1 Peter 4:17-19 says, the church is not exempt from the judgement, and we need to open ourselves to the light of God's examination. Judgment is not condemnation, nor primarily punishment. Condemnation, judgement, and punishment are only warranted, needed, and applied when they are warranted. The priority is to test and examine whether we are who we say we are, fraudulent or are found wanting.

This leads to our final section, "Doing;" doing something about what we described. We do this in relation to Jamaican and global society.

Doing

What can be done? What can the church do? I want to list several things the church can do to impact society.

Recognising the situation & Repenting from Self-Centredness and Sinfulness

First, the church needs to recognise the situation and repent of sinfulness and self-centeredness. We need to wake up and realize we live in a critical time. Not putting our heads in the sand like ostriches and hiding but recognize the situation around us. Communities are breaking up, people are losing their mental balance, and COVID-19 has ravaged people's health, education, and livelihood. Crime and corruption, particularly homicide and white-collar crime, stalk the land and are increasingly seen in many quarters as normal.

Capital is driving the society and the world. Not just buying, selling, and trading. Not just regular moneymaking. We have a market driven, capital economy and society where everything is related to making money. Time, energy, right and wrong, even relationships, are often subordinate or seen to be subordinate to making money.

We need to recognize this is the situation and the church's response is relatively ineffective. We are not touching these fundamental things but are skirting around them. We need to recognise the situation and repent of self-centredness and sinfulness and turn to God for help. Important, because crime and corruption, character and community fragmentation in a

capital-driven society are driven by self-centredness, producing sinfulness that is accumulative and devastating.

People are interested in "me, myself and I," and "what I can get rather what I can give." Some people are more interested in money than in people. The love of money is replacing the love of God. We need to turn away from such attitudes and actions and turn to Almighty God for help, the God of Jesus Christ.

Which leads us to our second point.

Receiving the Forgiveness, Deliverance, Salvation, Grace, Healing and Hope from God

We need to receive forgiveness, deliverance, salvation, healing, and the hope of God through Jesus Christ and become renewed regularly by the Holy Spirit of Jesus. All of these are important. Forgiveness of our sinful ways, deliverance from our self-centredness, salvation that we may be made whole with God and with ourselves and others, healing of our bodies, minds and spirits and hope for a better future. We need that desperately to ensure our people hear the gospel and receive its benefits by the grace of God. People desperately need to know they can be forgiven and delivered from those things that save from sin and for righteousness, healed in body, mind and spirit with hope for a better future.

This is possible through Christ who comes to give us life and have it more abundantly. We need to invite more people in and expect more people to come in. Though many might refuse, many might receive. We need to experience this as a daily reality and become renewed by the Holy Spirit of Jesus.

Perhaps some of us are jaded. "I'm tired and weary." One understands. But the Lord says He renews every day. Outwardly we might be wearing away, but inwardly we can be renewed every day by the Holy Spirit of Jesus. We need to ask God for that.

Restoring Relationships and Rebuilding Community
Thirdly, as a church, restore relationships with others and rebuild community. This is fundamentally what forgiveness is. We receive deliverance, salvation, healing, hope, and renewal. Not just for us but to have renewed and restored relationships with others. Sin breaks relationships, or makes them superficial, manipulative, or exploitative.

Changed and renewed, we receive salvation and the entire package from the Lord. By God's grace our relationships with others are restored. When God's Spirit works in us, the result, according to Galatians 5, is the fruit of the Spirit – love, joy, peace, patience, kindness, goodness, meekness, and self-control. These things are not virtues in themselves but are values and attitudes in relationship with others. These help us relate to others. Relationships require attention. We must be deliberate and intentional. We start within the body of Christ, with our brothers and sisters, but move out into families and circles of friends in all spheres of influence, whether at the workplace, school, or the wider community. We need to touch the wider community. At the heart of many fragmented situations in Jamaica and elsewhere is that people don't relate well to one another. Sadly, many Christians are guilty of relating badly. We need to change. Repentance, receiving salvation, and renewal by the Spirit must show in how we relate

to others; intentionally and deliberately being loving, kind, patient, peaceful; deliberately rebuilding community. Community means come-unity, to have oneness with others, to have healthy relationships.

This leads to what the church can do.

Reactivating Neighbourliness and Releasing Reparative Justice, Mercy, and Humility

We need to reactivate neighbourliness and release reparative justice, mercy, and humility into the wider society. Neighbourliness recognises the person who is in need that we should share life with and minister to. We should make it our aim to do so.

The story in Luke 10:25-37, about the Good Samaritan comes to mind. A Jewish man is on his way from Jerusalem to Jericho and was nearly killed by thieves who robbed him. The priests and Levites, members of the worship team of the day, passed him by. They were Jewish and he was Jewish. But it was a Samaritan who stopped to help him. Jesus' reason for telling that story was because a person from the worship team and religious leadership asked which commandment is the greatest. Jesus says you know what it is. The man answers yes: love the Lord with all your heart, soul, mind, and strength. The second is to love your neighbour as yourself. After Jesus tells him do this and you will live, the man asked Jesus, "but who is my neighbour?" Jesus tells him the story and asks the man, "who was neighbour to the man?" Not who is my neighbour, but who was neighbour to the man. That is still the question we need to answer: Who are we neighbour to? What does it mean to be a neighbour? The word comes from a Middle English

word that means "the one that is nearby." It is not just nearby physically, but the one who we are nearby in affection to, one who touches our heart. Which person or group of persons, or which kind of person, touch our heart. Those are the persons we are called to be near to and reach out to in the name of Jesus. Through his Spirit, and as part of his church, make a difference in the lives of such people. In so doing we fulfil God's commands. Therefore, we need to emphasize neighbourliness. There was a time when we were a much more neighbourly people before we were afflicted with corruption, crime, and community and character fragmentation. We need to release reparative justice, mercy, and humility. "Reparative" comes from a Latin word that means "to repair." A lot of things need to be repaired: relationships, people's economic standing, people's minds, people's social well-being, people's physical frames, people's infrastructure. We live in a country that is owed reparations from those who formerly colonized us. That fight continues and we need more people to join the fight. But in the meantime, what can we do?

We must release the reparations of justice, mercy, and humility in our society. Many people need reparative justice and be treated fairly, such as getting a living wage. We should support an increase in the minimum wage and ensure prices are not out of the range of people, whether to purchase everyday items or to pay utilities. We need to release the reparation of mercy, i.e., compassion to tell people, *the Living God cares for you, and I feel what you are feeling. I want to help repair some of the damage.* We need more people to help with counselling and deliverance so people oppressed by the devil and his works can find release and relief in their suffering.

Our brothers and sisters need that urgently. Especially in these COVID times, many people have just folded under and many more are on the edge. How can we send someone to school, make sure somebody eats, that people find basic medicine? We need that while we advocate for the powers-that-be to change economic policy so that justice can prevail. Mercy should continue. We seek justice and mercy. Both go together like rice and peas.

We should do that humbly before and with God. Micah 6:8 says God requires us to do justice, to love mercy and to walk humbly with our God. We should not be haughty, prideful, bombastic, behaving as if we are gods of the little tin pan variety. Rather, we should be like the God of Jesus Christ, who though He has great power and might, emptied Himself and became a servant. That is needed now. We need to release reparative service. Leaders are alienated from the people who they talk down to. They expect obedience without question. Their word is law, giving themselves titles. That God speaks through them, that they are gods themselves. Nothing could be further from the truth. Jesus humbled Himself, washed the feet of his disciples, fed them, cried with them, accompanied them, listened to them, learned from them, and learned from others. It is time we follow Jesus in humility. People will know we are His disciples. Love is the essence of justice, mercy, and humility, which makes a difference in the lives of others.

Revisiting and Rehabilitating the Free Village Strategy
That leads us to revisiting and rehabilitating of the free village strategy.

It was the church in Jamaica that provided a way for formerly enslaved African peoples after emancipation in 1834. The church, led by Baptists and Moravians, purchased plantations or land surrounding plantations to create Freedom Villages. These villages consisted of small acre plots that surrounded a central area where a church was built. These free villages operated on several levels.

They were economic units where the newly freed peasant worked the land for their families, buying, selling, and trading the crops grown to look after their households. They could be economically independent of the plantation life they were once a part of. These free villages were social units, as people interacted with each other without a master or overseers. They enjoyed the freedom they were given and fought for, without undue interference.

These free villages were political units, carved out in minimum one-acre plots so each person or family could vote in the country's parliament or assembly. The planter class felt threatened by this strategy and took the unprecedented step to suspend parliament and elections. Elections were not held until 1839, when they changed the rules that people needed to own ten acres of land to vote. The planter class disfranchised the peasantry, which contributed to the Morant Bay Uprising and other social and political protests in 19th century Jamaica. The church recognized it needed to change the political process and got involved.

The free village was also an educational, ideological, and religious unit. Educational, because it taught people to read, write and do arithmetic. Church schools started on Sundays in the church buildings after worship services. Many church

schools were started to meet the growing numbers of people needing the church's educational program. The church continues to play a key role in educating people in and from this country, a legacy of the free village movement. The free village was also religious. It emphasized learning to read the Bible, meeting the God of the Bible, and helping people become followers of Jesus Christ. The Christian foundation of Jamaica continued for the next 150 years. It began to change in radical ways in the 1990s because of the impact of globalization.

The free villages were ideological projects. They enabled the formerly enslaved to think of themselves as free. Free in Jesus and free because of Jesus and their efforts. Free because the church made a difference in their lives by fighting for freedom through persons such as Sam Sharpe and fighting to maintain freedom through others such as George William Gordon and Paul Bogle. The history of these Freedom Villages is largely forgotten, and their significance is largely undervalued. It is time to remember that history and reactivate it to help the fragmented communities and characters. We need a plan and strategy, and we have a blueprint: the free village system.

We cannot replicate the system exactly. Time has passed and the context is radically different. When the free villages started Jamaica was largely rural. Up to the eve of independence in 1962, Jamaica was 75 percent rural and 25 percent urban. In 1992, 30 years later, it was the opposite, 25 percent rural and 75 percent urban.

Thirty years later from 1992 and 60 years later from 1962, those distinctions are largely lost, thanks to the greater

connectivity with one another via developments and technologies. Roads, cell phones, talk shows and television programs, Internet, YouTube, and social media. People in the rural area can, in an instant, connect with someone in the city, for better or for worse. Not only in Jamaica but in towns, cities, and places across the world. In other words, Jamaica is increasingly urbanized, and its mindset citified, even in rural areas. Meanwhile, people in cities such as Kingston, Portmore, Ocho Rios, and Montego Bay, want to live the country life, aka natural life, shown in the foods they eat or the music they listen.

So, the free village strategy must be updated. In what ways? A detailed outline of the strategy is beyond the scope of this book. But we can give broad outlines. We need something that is economically helpful, enabling persons to earn incomes and be independent of dominant global and local capital. They need to buy, sell and trade in ways that preserve their dignity, independence and ability to determine their own destinies.

We need a strategy to help people socially, to relate to one another in community in ways that are mutually beneficial to all.

Even in depressed communities, there is much mutual interaction that is helpful. But because of persistent poverty, such interactions are often skewed and socially unhelpful. We need such communities, rural and urban, to enable people to help their neighbour and to receive help from that neighbour. This updated free village strategy needs a political component that empowers people and not keep them dependent on the party, politician or on the dons.

Once upon a time, the church was an important organization in a community, helping people to find jobs, educational opportunities, and move up the social ladder. This role is now played by politicians, dons, and gangs. The church needs to work with parties, politicians, and gangs for more horizontal nonpartisan approaches for human flourishing. But the church must also work with civil society for the wellbeing of our citizens, otherwise its influence will continue to diminish. The church must continue its role in charity, education, health, and skills training, at all levels. But it must go beyond these to provide liberty and transformative ways to affect the entire society, including encouraging those who are wealthier to share more of their goods and services with others, and not working only with the poor.

The church needs to tie these as well to the psychological, ideological, and religious (spiritual), because all are important to a holistic ministry. We need a vision of freedom – body, mind, spirit, economic, political, and societal – as our ancestors did. We bring them into God's holiness and wholeness, for the religious must be practical, not merely theoretical. Salvation, healing, and deliverance needs to move from people's words into people's lives, faith and need to affect their daily lives and vice versa. That is the Jesus way.

Reclaiming the Prophetic, Priestly and Pastoral Ministry of the Church

That leads us to reclaiming the prophetic, priestly, and pastoral ministries of the church, important to doing something about the signs we are reading. There is need for servant leadership that is prophetic, priestly, and pastoral.

The prophetic speaks for the Lord in the present based on the past and God's ways in the past, helping people navigate a new future. Prophesy is not merely speaking about the future, foretelling; it is speaking the truth to power in the present, forth telling. Saying thus saith the Lord, this is what the Lord says now. Prophets need to be aware of current events but read them in light of the ways of God, as seen in Scripture and in the history of the church. We need to be familiar with how God worked through the history of Caribbean people and the Caribbean church to learn from that history to guide people into the future that God has for them.

God's servant leaders are priests, praying to God on behalf of the people and hearing from God on behalf of the people. Bringing the people and their concerns to God and who bring God's concerns to the people.

Priests are intercessors and prophets need to be intercessors. Servant leadership in the church needs to be pastoral, caring for God's people, having them in our heart. We care for those gathered in congregations and for those scattered outside the church. We need to rescue the perishing and care for the dying. It is an honour and privilege to be a pastor, even as it is a great burden and responsibility. We need to take it seriously because the future of people, our country and its impact in the world, depends on it. My prayer is that servant leaders recommit and reaffirm their calling in Christ. We need to be priests, prophets, and pastors.

Remembering and Re-Membering the God-given Calling of the Jamaican People

This leads us to our final suggestion, to remember and re-member the God-given calling of the Jamaican people. When 60 years ago we were given a national pledge, among other things it said we as God's Jamaican people, pledge the love and loyalty of our hearts, the wisdom and courage of our minds and the strength and vigour of our bodies in the service of our fellow citizens. We promised to stand up for justice, brotherhood (solidarity) and peace, to work diligently and creatively, to think generously and honestly. We would do this, we said, so Jamaica would, under God, increase in fellowship, beauty, and prosperity, and play our part in advancing the welfare of the whole human race.

That was our pledge that we repeat every year since. But do we mean it when we hear it or say it? Do we understand it as a God-given calling as a people?

It is one reason why God raised us up as a distinct people. We are making a pledge before God and humanity. God hears and others hear what we have said. God takes us seriously. Ecclesiastes 5:1-7, says it is better not to pledge than to pledge and not keep the promise. Jamaicans say that a promise is a comfort to a fool, but God is no fool. God takes our promise seriously. I challenge us to remember the promise we made and are making to God and other people, especially in this 60th year of Jamaica's political independence.

We ought to remember the promise to love our people, to be loyal to them wherever we are, in Jamaica and around the world. We should be wise and courageous with our minds, and to use our strength to serve our fellow citizens. That we make

and keep the promise to stand up for justice, solidarity with our brothers and sisters, and for peace within our lives, society and communities.

We promise to work diligently and creatively in ways that are a blessing with the God-given gifts we have; to work diligently and honestly and give generously. We do this so that as Jamaicans, we enable our country and its people to increase in beauty and fellowship, so that Jamaica will (again) be a place that people will want to come to, not run from, when people see how we treat one another. Jamaica (again) would be prosperous materially, socially, economically, psychologically, religiously, and spiritually. We will, as a result, play our part to ensure the world fulfils its own promise.

This is a noble ideal. Because it is, we might fall short, but we should nevertheless aim for it. If we aim at nothing, we will hit it every time. If we aim at the sky, we may land on the mountains. I urge you, in this 60th year of Jamaica's independence, that we fulfil and remember our God-given calling as Jamaican people.

Summary

We were asked by the Lord to read the signs of the time, to recognize them; to understand what the present time is about and to do what is right in it and because of it. Reading those signs in the context of present-day Jamaica, we see many things happening. Some good, some bad.

We see concrete construction, constructive development, uncontrolled confidence, things being built and technology spreading. People are more connected and there is a deeper confidence in who we are as a people; in our art, speech, looks, and cultural forms. But that comes with a contradiction. We have much to celebrate, but are a people beset by crime and corruption, especially homicides and white-collar crimes. It is all over, some believing it is endemic.

We see that Jamaica is a Capital-Driven Society, where making money for a few, at the expense of everything and everyone, is paramount. There is community and character fragmentation with the penetration of capital into many communities, causing communities to break down and people to lose their social connection. This is contributing to a climate crisis, where natural hazards become disasters. The place where we live is not as safe and healthy as it was, evident in the COVID-19 pandemic, both its inception and in its handing, in how people related to and reacted to it.

We see that the church is relatively ineffective. While the church tries to meet the social and spiritual needs of people, deeper political, economic, psychological, and spiritual needs of people are not being met. We asked, why was this? We

discerned that Jamaica, like many places, is reaping the legacy of international colonialism when it was subjugated for 300 years by others. That ownership and what was extracted left us poorer.

Even though we have been independent the last 60 years, we are part of a world interconnected by imperialism. More than ever, we are connected one to the other, both within and outside societies. But we are not connected fairly. A few control the wealth of the world and the many are left with little to nothing. That is mirrored in local situations. Consequently, there is inequality and inequity; inequality because there are gaps between peoples' incomes and wealth; inequity because people are consistently and persistently disadvantaged by others who consistently and persistently have the advantage. There is great injustice and iniquity; injustice because people are treated unfairly; iniquity because people react to their unfair treatment by treating other people unfairly, as seen in criminal and corrupt activities.

In reaction, there is indifference as people do not care about others. Their needs come first, which is idolatry. Their demands, goods, services, achievements, and new acquisitions are gods that they worship. The Living God becomes an adjunct, a means to having and to keeping what is acquired.

People, in effect, are worshiping themselves and not the Living God. We need to ask God to help us overcome this idolatry because there is an identity crisis. We, as people in general and the church, do not know who we are and whose we are, that we belong to the Living God through Christ by the Spirit. That we ought to follow Him, because we will give

an account to Him for the life we live, individually and as nations.

Reading and relating Jesus' context in the 1st century C.E. to ours in the 21st century C.E., I believe, with all my heart, that we are facing imminent judgment. By judgment we don't mean punishment or condemnation, catastrophe, or disaster. We mean an examination. That God is looking at who we are, what we are about, and what we say. Just as a teacher tests if students are wasting their time in class, so the Lord sees whether we are Jesus' followers, seeking first His kingdom and His righteousness, or whether it is only about our own little fiefdom or agendas. The Lord is looking and examining. The question is whether we come up wanting or are passing the test.

Either way, there is work to do. Reading the signs of the time is describing or discerning and doing something about what we see.

We should, first, repent of our self-centredness, which accumulates sinfulness. Secondly, we need to receive the forgiveness and deliverance from bondage, the salvation that makes us whole, the healing that gives us strength, and the wisdom and hope of a better future. These are promises from God through Christ. We can all be renewed day by day by the Holy Spirit of Jesus, become more and receive more of what God would have us to be, do and possess.

We need to ask God's help to restore relationships with others, as we relate to them through the Spirit in more loving, kind, patient, self-control, meek, good, and helpful ways that rebuild community; that make us more unified, more whole

and more together, to counter the character and community fragmentation that is prevalent.

God calls us to exhibit the spirit of neighbourliness, to get connected to those in need, to draw near to them, and to minister to them. We do this by releasing reparative justice, mercy, and humility, to repair the damage that many people experienced because of living in an oppressive system. We need to treat people fairly and ensure they are treated fairly, singularly, and collectively, through personal interactions and public policies. We ought to exercise mercy and compassion for people as we also need mercy from God. People are not perfect; some are simple and others wicked. But if they turn and are in need, mercy should be extended. We should act justly and compassionately, in humility with God, remembering we are not gods. We are creatures of God, servants of God and will have to give an account to God for our lives.

We need, at the bigger, wider, and deeper levels, to revisit the free village strategy. To find economic, social, political, educational, psychological, ideological, and religious ways to have people be free. Free from oppression and to determine their lives under God; to live to full potential as human beings and communities. This requires reclaiming the prophetic, priestly, and pastoral ministries of the church. Revisiting the role of servant leaders in the church and community on which the backbone of the church and the country was built. This is called for. But we must remember we are not to lord it over people but assist and help them to be all that God called them to be.

God is calling us to remember and re-member the God-given calling of the Jamaican people; to live the life we should so Jamaica may, under God, increase in beauty, fellowship and prosperity and play her part in advancing the welfare of the whole human race.